Sarah Mather
and Underwater Telescopes

By Ellen Labrecque

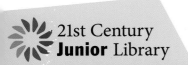
21st Century
Junior Library

Published in the United States of America by
Cherry Lake Publishing
Ann Arbor, Michigan
www.cherrylakepublishing.com

Content Adviser: Amelia Wenk Gotwals, Ph.D., Associate Professor of Science Education, Michigan State University
Reading Adviser: Marla Conn MS, Ed., Literacy specialist, Read-Ability, Inc.

Photo Credits: © Tischenko Irina/Shutterstock Images, cover; © L.Fabre/CEA, 4; © North Wind Picture Archives/Alamy Stock Photo, 6; © US National Archives Records Administration, 8; © Lonnie Gorsline/Shutterstock Images, 10; © Everett Historical/Shutterstock Images, 12; © Educational Insights, 14; © NOAA Office of Ocean Exploration and Research, 16; © sbelov/iStock, 18; © Bates Littlehales/Contributor/Getty Images, 20

Library of Congress Cataloging-in-Publication Data
Names: Labrecque, Ellen, author.
Title: Sarah Mather and underwater telescopes / by Ellen Labrecque.
Description: Ann Arbor, Michigan : Cherry Lake Publishing, [2017] | Series: 21st century junior library. Women innovators |
    Audience: K to grade 3. | Includes bibliographical references and index.
Identifiers: LCCN 2016029710 | ISBN 9781634721813 (hardcover) | ISBN 9781634723138 (pbk.) |
    ISBN 9781634722476 (pdf) | ISBN 9781634723794 (ebook)
Subjects: LCSH: Mather, Sarah—Juvenile literature. | Women inventors—United States—Biography—Juvenile literature. |
    Underwater exploration—History—Juvenile literature.
Classification: LCC T40.M275 L33 2017 | DDC 551.46092—dc23
LC record available at https://lccn.loc.gov/2016029710

Cherry Lake Publishing would like to acknowledge the work of The Partnership for 21st Century Skills.
Please visit *www.p21.org* for more information.

Printed in the United States of America
Corporate Graphics

CONTENTS

Underwater telescopes are used by scientists to study the ocean.

A Woman

Have you ever used a **telescope** to look at the stars? Telescopes can help you see deep into space. Did you also know that telescopes can be used to look deep into the ocean?

Sarah Mather invented the world's first underwater telescope. Mather lived more than 200 years ago. Thanks to her **invention**, scientists today continue to explore the ocean with telescopes!

We do not know very much about Sarah Mather's life,
but she did live in Brooklyn, New York.

Sarah Porter Stiman was born in New York in 1796. Not much is known about her parents or what her childhood was like. But in 1819, when she was 23, Stiman married Harlow Mather. They lived in Brooklyn, New York.

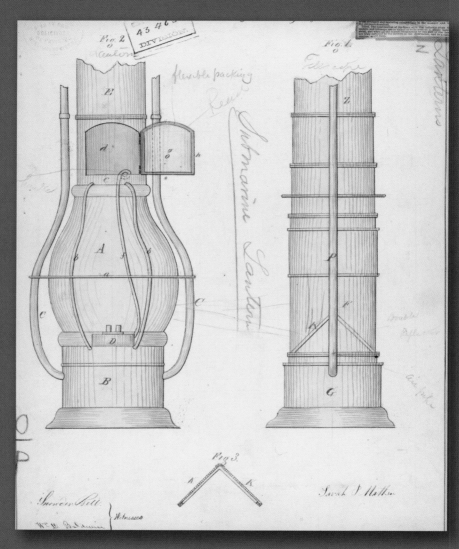

To get a patent, Mather made detailed
drawings of her invention.

An Idea

On April 16, 1845, Mather was granted a **patent** for an invention. She called it the **submarine** telescope. The telescope could "examine objects under the surface of the water." She described it as a tube with a bright light attached.

Mather's invention was used for many different purposes.

The telescope allowed people to see 250 feet (76 meters) below the water and as far as 500 feet (152 m) in any direction. Scientists could use Mather's telescope to study fish. Explorers could find sunken ships. Sailors could examine ships for damage. People said Mather's invention was more helpful than the telescope used to look at stars!

Think!

Why did Mather's invention need a light attached to it?
Do oceans get darker the deeper they go? Why or why not?

Mather's invention was very important to the North during the Civil War.

Mather's telescope even helped save lives. From 1861 to 1865, the United States was fighting the Civil War. The fighting was between the North and the South. The North used Mather's telescope to detect the South's underwater warships. The South couldn't launch surprise attacks on the North. The North was ready! Mather's telescope was described as having "great importance to the Navy and to navigators throughout the world."

Today, there are underwater telescopes designed for kids.

A Legacy

Mather died on June 21, 1868, at age 72. Her **legacy** was her invention. It changed the way we see below the sea. Today, improved telescopes and underwater cameras allow scientists to continue making discoveries. With more than 70 percent of Earth covered in water, there are still lots of underwater places left to explore.

The *Okeanos Explorer* was used in the 2016
Deepwater Exploration of the Marianas expedition.

The Marianas Trench is located 7 miles (11 kilometers) below the earth's surface in the Pacific Ocean. It is the deepest part of the ocean. In the summer of 2016, underwater cameras documented an exploration of the region. People around the world were able to watch a live view of the ocean floor on the Web.

Create!

What do you think the Marianas Trench looks like? What creatures do you think you would see there? Draw a picture of what you imagine. Look up photos and videos online. Does your picture match what you find? What is the same? What is different?

New underwater telescopes can help scientists
make important discoveries in places like Lake Baikal.

Underwater telescope **technology** has also continued to **evolve**. Lake Baikal in Russia is the biggest and deepest freshwater lake in the world. Scientists use a special underwater telescope to study the lake. They aren't looking for fish or underwater plants. They are looking for **particles** that could show how the universe was formed!

Mather's invention allowed people to see the ocean floor for the first time.

Without Mather's invention over 170 years ago, none of this would have been possible! Mather gave the world its first look at the dark ocean depths. She might not have imagined all the ways her invention could be used after she created it. However, her resourceful creativity made her a true inventor!

Look!

Check out this image of an underwater telescope. How is it similar to a regular telescope? How is it different?

GLOSSARY

evolve (ih-VAHLV) to develop and change as a result of many small steps

invention (in-VEN-shun) something new created from imagination

legacy (LEG-uh-see) something handed down from one generation to another

particles (PAHR-ti-kuhlz) extremely small pieces of something

patent (PAT-uhnt) the right granted by the government to use or sell an invention for a certain number of years

submarine (suhb-muh-REEN) a vessel that moves and operates under the surface of the water instead of on top of it

technology (tek-NAH-luh-jee) the use of science in industry or engineering to invent useful things or solve problems

telescope (TEL-uh-skope) a device that makes objects appear bigger and closer than they really are

FIND OUT MORE

BOOKS

Greenblatt, Jacquelyn. *Women Scientists and Inventors: A Science Puzzle Book*. Glenview, IL: Good Year Books, 1999.

MacQuitty, Miranda. *Ocean*. New York: DK Publishing, 2014.

Thimmesh, Catherine. *Girls Think of Everything: Stories of Ingenious Inventions by Women*. New York: HMH Books for Young Readers, 2002.

WEB SITES

Famous Women Inventors
www.women-inventors.com
Learn more about women inventors in history.

National Geographic—Deepsea Challenge 3D
www.deepseachallenge.com/
Learn about how we are exploring underneath the sea today.

INDEX

ABOUT THE AUTHOR

Ellen Labrecque is a freelance writer living in Yardley, Pennsylvania. Previously, she was a senior editor at Sports Illustrated Kids. Ellen loves to travel and then learn about new places and people that she can write about in her books.